Seeing in the Dark

**Poems and Reflections
for when
Life Gets Tough**

Hilary Allen

ISBN: 978-1-907929-64-9

You can contact Hilary Allen at:seeinginthedark824@gmail.com

Lp

www.lifepublications.org.uk

Dedication

To all those with whom I have journeyed sharing our joys and tears.

Commendations

We have all experienced dark times. Times when life doesn't seem to be following the plan we had. Times when we walk with others who are struggling in their own darkness. This collection of poems is for anyone who knows what dark times are and for those who are seeking encouragement and closeness to God, the only provider of unfailing hope and security.

Hilary has drawn on her considerable life experience as a family doctor, daughter and friend to many, and ultimately as a person who understands what darkness is for herself and others.

Be inspired, challenged, comforted and draw closer to God as you read and ponder this unique collection of verse.

Janet Gillett
Palliative care physician

These poems are a blessing. A touching reminder of the love, care and embrace of God. Vivid imagery which lingers in the mind and heart. Food and light for the soul, especially in the dark and confusing corners of life. Breathing deeply of Hilary's words brings the peace of God which passes all understanding.

Rev William Lane c/SSF
Vicar and fellow Street Pastor

The author has produced a thought-provoking collection of reflections and poems which remind and encourage me in the knowledge and promise that Jesus is with me now, always, whatever the challenge or joy that I encounter. He never leaves me although I often leave Him.

In this book, Hilary gives us the affirmation of hope and trust in a loving God who takes us gently by the hand as we, in our human frailty, cautiously step forward into the dark, confident that we are safe, loved, heard, strong.

I encountered this book at a time of intense grief following the death of my husband. I felt lost and felt very alone, although I did not lack company. My confidence was shattered and I was seeking answers to questions that I myself was not sure what I was asking.

This book brings me support and an ability to believe in myself, in my future, in my place on this earth as a human being. It is a book of support and caring. Hilary reaches out and touches the heart with her poems. It is a book for all who seek to know more of life, of love, of stepping forward, of themselves. I thoroughly recommend it.

Annette Griffiths

Informed by a lifetime's experience of human emotions, Hilary has woven a rich tapestry of poetry embracing poignancy and compassion. Her writing is enriched with a refreshing honesty about matters of eternal significance which gently challenge the listener to reflect and respond.

Adrian Prior-Sankey MBE

This collection of poems will bring hope, comfort and inspiration to anyone experiencing moments of worry, self-doubt or fear of the present or future. Hilary's strong faith shines through and I love the way the poems end on a note of positivity that the answer is always found in our Father God.

In particular the poem *Do You Know?* really resonates and is one to which I return time and time again.

I thoroughly recommend taking a few moments to read these when life gets tough, for we are all held in the palm of God's hand.

Jenny Patten

Hilary writes poems from the heart. She covers topics of everyday life and everyday struggles for meaning, hope and joy. In her search she finds the quiet beauty of nature, the sustaining strength in friendships and the elusive yet ever present love of God. People who are looking for inspiration, comfort and connection will find nourishment for their souls in Hilary's poems.

The Rev'd. Robin Pfaff
Chaplaincy Team-Leader for Community and Mental Health
Somerset NHS FT

Have you ever asked, "God, will you show me where you are in this?" I have. This collection of writing speaks to the heart, encouraging me to know God's presence and His love for me in every moment of life.

As you dip into this book be refreshed, re-centred and reassured that God is with you always.

Sue Cooper

Contents

From the Author

My work as a GP, voluntary Pastoral support, Street Pastor and
Hospital Chaplain, has brought me alongside the hurting, the
confused, the bereaved and the questioning.
This collection of poetry is an exploration of finding God in the
stuff of each of our lives. Be encouraged and strengthened in
faith, because God is always waiting to share His heart.

Hilary

*Please see the Appendix (p 57) at the back to find footnotes for further
reflection and also the background to many of the poems.*

The Love of God

The love of God is beauty
            joy
            powerful
            holy
            tender
            passionate
            strong
            safe
            dynamic
            daring
            breaking all limits
            leading
            teaching
            healing
            advocacy
            moving into wholeness
            unconditional
            never a cross word
            forgiveness
            touching Him
            and not being separated.

The love of God is.

Distance

I've kept my distance,
yet I've wondered why You seemed so remote,
just pie in the sky.
I've always feared the demands You'd make;
would You change my life, happiness forsake?
You're my arms-length Saviour,
kept just in case my helter-skelter world
forgets Your grace.
But I know one day that my life will end;
when I meet You then, will You call me friend?
Will You point to Your cross and sin's defeat,
crying, "This the cost to make you complete.
Was it really in vain for you I died?"
And all that I see
are Your arms stretched wide.

You

You do not have to prove your worth
with striving or success.
It's not by always doing more
that I will be impressed.
Your worth, My child, is in My love;
Precious, priceless, unique;
I cherish and refine with care
unstinting, 'til complete.
And I don't see the stains that mar
since My Son paid your price:
All that I see, through tears of joy,
is that you've chosen Christ.

The Gift

The egret, stiletto-heeled, tiptoes into the estuary flow,
then statuesque, awaits its early catch.
Scurrying dunlins peck incessantly at the tidal fringe
beyond the stranded seaweed carpeting the shore.
A solitary snail stretches, edging to
the puddle's distant reach.
Each, journeying, receives
the gift of the new day.

Reaching Down

God,
You reach down
from the Heavens
to give the gift of today
to bless me
to comfort me
to take my hand
to love me.
To be with me
to be my joy
to be my hope
to cherish me
to ask me
to follow You
to take risks for You.
Thank you for loving me so much.

Cobwebs on the Cross

You haven't been here lately
there are cobwebs on the cross!
You've lived your life without My grace
and struggled on your own.
Kept up appearances but lost My joy.
Dutifully wearied on
a stranger to My face.
Said you'd manage; didn't need Me,
hadn't time to spend apart.
Too tired to make the effort
you drifted in the dark.
Do you not know you cannot live
My way all on your own?
Come, write your name here in the dust,
on priceless wood that bore all sin and pain.
Weep tears of need that wash away
your pride and self-sufficiency.
Come, write your name.

The Lake

The lake was still, tranquil in the morning light.
I, too, was still, watching and listening.
What would God say to me today?

A dragonfly danced and darted,
busy, active, distracted,
then rested beside me,
amber-iridescent in the sun.
Being not doing.

God said I could be like that,
being not doing,
receiving His love.

The Peace of God

Let the peace of God
comfort you.
Let the hand of God
hold and sustain you.
Let the grace of God
transform you.
Let the blessing of God Almighty
encourage you
give you hope
each day.

18

Be

Be still
Be
Before My presence
Be
Beyond concerns
Be
Be calm, at peace
Be
Be known to Me
Be
Believe in Me
Be
Behold I AM
Be
Beloved, precious
Be
Become
Be
Being with Me.

Do You Know?

Do you know
    that you are loved
        just where you are?
Do you know
    that I understand
        just where you are?
Do you know
    you are held safe
        just where you are?
Do you know
    I seek your heart
        just where you are?
Do you know
    I dwell with you
        just where you are?

I will seek You

My hands are empty
my heart is cold.
I do not have
all You have promised.
God in the silence,
God in my darkness,
God in the distance,
God, You are always kind,
always sure,
always loving.
I will seek You,
I will kneel before You.
My hands are open
my heart is opened.
God I trust,
for with You
is eternal life.

I AM

I AM	the bread that you need
I AM	the light that you need
I AM	the truth that you long to find.
I AM	the grace that you need
I AM	the strength that you need
I AM	the guide that you long to find.
I AM	the mercy that you need
I AM	the salvation that you need
I AM	the peace that you long to find.
I AM	the freedom that you need
I AM	the love that you need
I AM	the life that you long to find.
I AM	the God that you long to find.

Janus

Two faces and two directions;
which of the stories define us?
The storms of life or the potential growth?
The doors now closed or pushing on open ones?
The never stepping out or the journeying?
The failures or the risk of trying again?
The sorrow and loss or the fresh discoveries?
Which of the stories define us?
The endings or the new beginnings?
The frozen fear or the heart-beat of freedom?
The lies we deny or the truths we own?
The bitterness we choose or the cultivation of love?
The feverish busyness or finding deep stillness?
Which of *our* stories defines us?

From Psalm 23
The Good Shepherd

Do you know   I am the good Shepherd
                      Always good, always kind?

Do you know   I am your helper
                      Always mindful, always attentive?

Do you know   I will carry you
                      even when your heart is faint?

Do you know   I will show you My way
                      Always sure, always wanting you
                      close?

Do you know   I will protect you
                      Always held, always safe?

Do you know   I will never leave you
                      even if you wander astray?

Do you know   I take great delight in you
                      Always cherished, always precious?

Do you know   I am all you need
                      Always providing, always blessing?

Do you know   I am constant in working for your
                      good
                      even in the darkness?

Do you know?

Psalm 139
How Precious

How precious Your thoughts of me O God,
How intimate Your care for me
How deep Your searching of my intent
How keenly You daily see.

How longing You desire I walk your path
How watchful of my life's deeds
How securely You hold in fear or loss
How knowing of all my needs.

How understanding when I slip and fall
How certain Your rescue comes
How fully Your grace restores my soul
How freely Your forgiveness runs.

How steadfast and good are all Your ways
How completely You work Your plan
How utterly faithful are Your promises
How accepted and loved I am.

How precious am I to You O God
How grateful we journey together
How gladly I open up my heart
To truly enjoy You for ever.

Luke 15

Jesus told stories to the religious content
So they would know Father's heart, Father's intent.
God's passion for the lost, His ultimate cost
Saving, restoring, love utterly spent.

The shepherd risked everything by seeking one sheep,
Courage and persistence on sheer rocky steeps.
His passion for the lost, accepting the cost;
Sheep rescued, his joy was complete.

The frantic housewife swept every floor, every quoin,
Tirelessly searching her precious wedding coin.
Her passion for the lost, whatever the cost,
Cherished finding, her dowry conjoins.

Faithful father whose love is unconditional
Fervently prays for a rescued prodigal.
His passion for the lost, the hurt of the cost!
His deep forgiveness immeasurable.

Jesus told stories to the religious content
So we would know Father's heart, Father's intent.
God's passion for the lost, His ultimate cost,
Challenging us how our lives should be spent.

God, do You still do it?

God do You still do it – do You still weep?
Over cities, homes, our sanitised streets?
The Bible says that You did long ago
but now, how on earth are we meant to know?

God do You cry at injustice and pain?
With those who never will be whole again?
God do You hate our greed and deceit
and God do You weep with those who can weep?

God do you walk in our world today?
See the drugs, violence, the social decay?
God does our suffering tear You apart?
The lost, abused – are they close to Your heart?

God what are You doing there in the sky?
Or is it despair which makes us yell 'why?'
You ask followers be Your hands, Your feet.
God may we know and show Your love so deep.

He Came

He came in the darkness.
Laid bare His scars, His wounds
and said He knew:
Knew the pain and loss, the disgrace and the
waste.
Knew the brokenness and hurt, the betrayal and
guilt.
Knew the aloneness and emptiness.
Knew how fear and anger could torture and
imprison.
He came into the darkness,
offered His own damaged hands, His butchered
feet, His spear-torn side.
He came to invite touch, truth, belief,
faith, trust, peace and healing.
"Stretch out *your* hands," He said,
"I AM."

Seeing in the Dark

I want to see in the darkness,
not stumble or cry with pain.
I want to know which way to take
not falter or tread in vain.
I want to trust familiar holds,
from unknown fears, safely kept.
I want to see in the darkness
but no one's succeeded yet.

There's One who guides in the darkness,
unseen, yet sure is His hold.
Close when it seems too much to bear,
insisting He carry my load.

Just Looking

When I look but do not see,
when I see but do not feel,
when I feel but do not think,
when I think but do not act,
when I act but do not love,
Lord, have mercy.

God's Arms

God, are your arms long enough
to reach deep down
in the hole
where I am?

> "My arms extend for ever
> to reach even
> to rock-bottom."

God, are your arms strong enough
to pull me out
and enfold me
in your care?

> "My arms are mighty
> to lift you up
> bringing you close to My heart.
> To wrap around you,
> around and around."

God is your love deep enough
to clasp me secure;
never left alone, but hidden,
cradled tight in your arms?

"I am God Almighty."

The Sea

I went to the sea in search of peace
for that special thought from You
to call my own.
My disappointment found
waves moody, turbulent and restless,
crashing unpredictably on the rocks,
showering splattered spray.
I longed for a tranquil, calming sea,
idyllic gentle waves lapping the shore;
A cosy reassurance of Yourself
to tuck into my fast-track life.
Instead, I gasped at sudden surge of surf,
mighty, ceaseless pounding waves,
wind that whipped the tossing tide.
In that moment,
awed by the sea's Creator,
I bowed;
a mere created one.

The Beach

Lord why do I always see
    the boulders and not the beach?
    The problems and not the promise?
    The hurt and not the hope?
    My failings and not my friend?

Grains of Sand

I count the grains of sand on the shore,
I know the number of hairs on your head,
the tears you weep for the pain you keep
and the restless nights on your bed.
I know what bothers you large and small;
if only you knew what I'd do!
I know the plans that I have conceived
taking care and delight in you.
Know that I formed your very being
and I watch every day as you grow;
so why so slow to love and trust?
I know. Yes, I know. Yes, I know.
You cannot change My heart to forget,
stop loving or ignore your plight.
I thought of you with My dying breath,
you are so precious in My sight.

Hope

The waves crash against the tiny rock.
I feel so small, almost submerged.
Powerless against the ceaseless tide of
demand,
of activity.
And all I can do
is to be still
and silent toward God,
realising anew
I'm anchored to Bedrock.

God is in the Silence

God is in the silence.
There in the emptiness
holding me close
counting my tears
feeling my pain
listening to my sorrow
healing the hurt
knowing my needs
breathing His peace
journeying with me
affirming me.
God is in the silence.

Like Grass

The mountains stood immovable,
carved fast; by tempest tried.
Resolute but barren. Solid. Defined.
Mountains endure.
Then You call
to watch the ballet of the grass
dancing in the breeze.
Velvet cloaks curtsying,
softly spinning,
free yet yielding.
Alive to life's adventure,
pliable, willing to be blown.
Imaging that You require
of me a soft heart.
Lord, may I never miss
the music of the dance.

Fruit of the Spirit

So did you think that in life's course the fruit would
naturally appear?
Just ready-picked and vacuum-packed,
without the husbandry of God working in partnership
with us?
Rooted in Him, by Him resourced,
the precious fruit will be produced, wherever we may
be planted.
Growth in each season of our lives;
through the Winter of our discontent,
or in Spring's new challenges and change,
in Summer's abundant, care-free days,
or in the Autumn of our passing years;
all give opportunity to blossom and to fruit.
So love is nurtured in the cold climate of the hurt and
hate.
Joy is cultivated when we accept Your gifts with
gratitude.
God's peace implanted in our storms
and patience perfected through prayer.
Goodness grown by each response and choice we

make in daily cares.
Kindness is crafted as we share each others' and each
stranger's needs.
Gentleness is germinated as we receive afresh God's
grace.
Self-control is trained through trial
and faith is grafted from our doubt.
So Holy Spirit, this my prayer would daily be,
"Come, produce Your fruit in me!"

Whatever

Whatever the weather,
Whatever I'm feeling,
Whatever my failure,
Whatever my fear,
God still loves me
God will never give up on me.
Whatever the conflict,
Whatever the terror,
Whatever the crisis,
Whatever the chaos,
God still loves me
God will never give up on me.
Whatever injustice,
Whatever changes,
Whatever sadness,
Whatever brings joy,
God still loves me
God will never give up on me.
Whatever you endure,
Whatever you plan,
Whatever you think,
Whatever you seek,
God still loves you
God will never give up on you. Whatever.

Beautiful Child

Beautiful child,
you are not defined by your failures,
you are not limited by your achievements,
you are not condemned by your omissions,
you are not burdened by your guilt or
   complicity.
Seek My forgiveness.
Let My grace come.
Allow My unconditional love to re-create.
Let go and forgive yourself.
My beautiful child,
to fully live
in the richness of My grace,
go and do likewise
for others.

The Path

It's all uphill;
wind blowing in my face,
dark clouds threatening in the sky:
I grit my teeth and wearily struggle on.
There is no firm hold;
feet slip and slide.
It's lonely.
What's the point?
I know You're there
but You're not here,
here where I am alone.
But then in reaching a different turn of the path
I see the vista of Your love;
that difficulties were lessons in trust
not abandonment.
Come close,
bathe me in the light of Your grace.
Warm me with the passion of Your care.
Then You, take my hand and hold me tight.
Let me follow where You lead,
even if the way is rough,
because we go together.

Openness

Limitless God,
the God of immeasurably more,
illume my vision,
that I may see Your unfailing goodness.
Soften my heart,
that I may receive Your steadfast love.
Nurture my trust,
that I may let go of all that holds me back.
Breathe Your peace,
that I may cease from worry.
Reveal Your words of truth,
that I may be set free.
Kindle my faith,
that I may be sure of Your promises.
Plant seeds of expectancy
that I may hope in Your purposes.
Speak into my soul,
that I may be Your risk-taker.
God without limits,
God of immeasurably more,
come.

The Pebble

You found the perfect pebble on the beach today;
complete, fully rounded, silky smooth.
A testimony of its journey,
its shaping by the sea:
Dashed by pounding surf,
thrown, hurled against hidden rocks,
rolled and rolled by ebbing tides,
trodden on by countless feet.
Yielding, always yielding to the powerful force of
sea.
Never broken, but eternally re-made.
A work of art.
In yielding to Creator God, you too
know surf and tide and tossing,
hurling and crushing.
And you too are re-made,
in God's image,
as His precious work of art.

Where is my Hope?

Hope is the appearance of morning light
    the rhythm and constancy of seasons
    seeing the rainbow through the rain
Hope is in the kindness of a friend.

Hope is peace amidst the storm
    the healing from forgiveness
    God making good in the darkness
Hope is the generosity of grace to me.

Hope is finding God comes close
    giving strength for today
    answering my prayer
Hope is God releasing gifts within.

Hope is knowing a God who wants me
    shaping me for His purposes
    transforming me into the likeness of
    Christ
Hope is experiencing God's power and His
    blessing.

Hope is rooted in God's faithfulness
    God's promises fulfilled
    the confidence of heaven
Hope is clinging to Him.

Will You?

Will you love Me in this?
My arms are strong tight around you.
I will safely carry you.
I will watch over you.
My love to overcome your fear
My courage through your tears
My comfort for your hope
My breath enabling each new day.
Truly, I am here with you
I am and always will be for you.
I can never let you down.
Nothing stops Me loving you.
So, will you love Me in this?

The Oyster Pearl

The grit, the grief,
the problem and the pain.
The ugly unexpected,
the annoyance.
Difficulty is not black or white
but subtle translucent layers;
glimpses of healing
imperceptibly forming
the pearl's beauty.
The oyster learns
a different way of being.

An Attitude of Gratitude

Father, nurture in me an attitude of gratitude,
not fleeting thankfulness nor platitudes,
but heartfelt response of such magnitude
in knowing I'm loved and cherished.

Father, nurture in me an attitude of gratitude,
for blessings of family, friends and food,
for nature's beauty and the season's moods,
for my freedom, hope and my peace renewed.

Father, nurture in me an attitude of gratitude,
for medicine and science secrets pursued,
for craft and art and music's plenitude,
for laughter, health and rest's beatitude.

Father, nurture in me an attitude of gratitude,
for leisure and work, skills and wealth accrued,
neither hoard nor begrudgingly extrude,
but share with the needy multitudes.

Father, nurture in me an attitude of gratitude,
that seeks Your will through prayerful solitude,
that gives of time in selfless servitude,
and so proves the Love I cherish.

Father, nurture in me such an attitude.

God's Time

Prayer is God's time for God's revealing
Prayer is God's space for God's speaking
Prayer is God's silence for our discovering
Prayer is God's comfort for our enabling
Prayer is God's forgiving for our freeing
Prayer is God's truth for our enlightening
Prayer is God's light for our directing
Prayer is God's breath for our infilling
Prayer is God's presence for our embracing
Prayer is God's love for our believing
Prayer is God's provision for our trusting
Prayer is God's power for our transforming
Prayer is God's listening for our affirming
Prayer is God's grace for our blessing
Prayer is God's heart shared for our responding
Prayer is God's time for God's glorifying.

Hurt

I'm angry. It isn't fair.
I've every right to hit back.
I relish my words,
savour the action I will take.
I allow the wounds to fester,
filling my mind
again and again.
Absorbed, justified, crushed.
I trigger the memories,
lick the pain,
feel the stinging soreness.
Then God asks, where is He?
Isn't He making me new?
Isn't this His work, not mine?
How can He change what I hold on to?

Mind the Gap

Lord, give to me the wisdom
to mind the gap in the waiting; in the 'not yet' time.
Give to me the desire to seek You in the silence.
Give to me the patience to listen for Your still, small
voice.
Give to me the blessing of Your presence in the
emptiness.
Give to me confidence in a God who holds me fast.
Give to me belief in the constant power of prayer.
Give to me the kindness of Your unfailing love.
Give to me the courage to cling to Your promises.
Give to me a strengthening of purpose to live well this
day.
Give to me Your sustaining in the darkness.
Give to me the willingness to receive Your healing.
Give to me Your rest in my sleeplessness.
Give to me a deepening trust in Your greater good.
Give to me a transformation of my heart, my mind.
Give to me obedience in the unfolding of Your will.
Give to me Your peace in every circumstance.

Rose

Rose
tight budded
unfolding with the Light
teach me this day
how to blossom.

The Cup

Lord, not *this* cup.

I don't want *this* cup!

Not the bitter cup of suffering;
of letting go of life,
of dying yet being alive,
of being used less and useless,
of losing control,
of watching energy wane
with weak weary struggle.
Of being torn from arms of love.
The aching fear,
the terror of the yet unknown,
the anguish of the pain,
the denial of dignity,
the aloneness,
the silence of awkward speech.
Not *this* cup!
The never seeing all I'd planned,
The never being all I am again.
The cup *is* in my hands, cold, stark.
So also is Your promised presence,
warm, close, whispering,
"Fear not, I am with you.
I have not let you go."

Walk Slowly

Walk slowly through the storm;
the wrecking, raging havoc.
Tread gently through the hopes and dreams
now savagely uprooted and for ever lost.
Bend low against the lashing wind,
wrapping kindness softly as a cloak around.
Drink the stillness of sadness,
let questions hang unanswered.
Cease words which stifle inner calm,
listen deeply to the silence of the heart.
Touch uncertainty, hold it's hand,
to ease each burden that you carry.
Look beyond the devastation, the broken debris
strewn,
know God is here and will console.
Embrace God's given strength afresh,
His presence in this day.
Wait and find
your own untrodden way.
Know vulnerability
and the letting go.

Will You Hold My Hand?

Will you hold My hand
let Me rescue you?
I forgive and accept completely.
Will you hold My hand?

Will you hold My hand
all life's journey through?
Use My gifts in service for others?
Will you hold My hand?

Will you hold My hand,
always love Me first?
Follow Me truly as I guide you?
Will you hold My hand?

Will you hold My hand
if you cry for help?
Seek My strength, My grace and My
presence?
Will you hold My hand?

Will you hold My hand
as blessings overflow,
mindful of Me in all life's fullness?
Will you hold My hand?

Will you hold My hand
speak out My truth,
love enemies as I commanded?
Will you hold My hand?

Will you hold My hand
go tell the world
God's love fully pardons and transforms?
Will you hold My hand?

Will you hold My hand
when you're all alone
with fears, or despair in your darkness?
Will you hold My hand?

Will you hold My hand
when loss overwhelms;
receive My steadfast care and healing?
Will you hold My hand?

Will you hold My hand
when death's shadow falls
and I cradle you Home for ever?
Will you hold My hand?

Stay Close

Stay close, you're not beyond My touch;
realise you're loved so very much.
Stay close, stop wandering away
and discipline yourself to pray.
Stay close, My promises are true,
take them to be fulfilled in you.
Stay close, I choose to walk with you;
invite Me in to all you do.
Stay close, despite feeling alone,
your every hurt is already known.
Stay close as problems make you fret;
I've seen the weight of tears you've wept.
Stay close when sorrow brings you low,
I'm holding you, I'll not let go.
Stay close if fear arrests your path,
My power and strength are yours to ask.
Stay close when stressed with little time,
know all the days and hours are Mine.
Stay close, feed on the words I spoke,
obey and live in certain hope.
Stay close and spend more time with Me,
My heart and purpose then you'll see.
Stay close, you're now My hands and feet,
bring My Kingdom to all you meet.

Stay close, your love for Me renew,
I never will give up on you.
Stay close and on your knees adore
I AM, your God, for evermore.

Stay with us Lord

"Stay with us Lord, the day is spent."
My day is spent.
I embrace God's presence into my present;
God is in the silence and in the clamour,
God is in my busyness and in my rest,
God is beyond but also here.
Stay with me, Lord.

Appendix

***An** Attitude of Gratitude*: Psalm 138:1. I'm not good at this. I recognize that I need to cultivate this attitude within me. My prayer is that God will help me not just today, but every day.

Be: Psalm 46:10. I have found it essential, but challenging, to find space to be, as I live life in the fast-lane. God graciously longs for us to be in His presence and never turns us away. Hear God tell you how much you mean to Him. How deeply you are loved.

Beautiful Child: Ephesians 1:3-8. The boundlessness of God's love, His forgiveness and care for each of us is simply indescribable. Translate this wonder into life today.

Cobwebs on the Cross: Psalm 86:5. Know for yourself God's kindness, His complete forgiveness and constant love.

Distance: Isaiah 30:15. My pre-conception of God or my past experience of religion or a father figure may keep me at a distance from God. Yet God loves each of us so very much and longs that we know Him.

Do You Know? Matthew 7:11. God's love is truly there for us. Discover the 'how much more' God gives as we journey with Him.

Fruit of the Spirit: Galatians 5:22-23. There's no pick and mix in how God continuously grows His life within us. In common with all cultivation, we need nurture and nourishment. How diligent is God's husbandry.

God, do You still do it? Isaiah 58:6-9. I wrote and performed this at a celebration of our local Street Pastors' 10th anniversary. It is an amazing privilege to be out on the streets at night, meeting people and sharing God's love in the reality and realism of their lives.

God's Arms: Psalm 40:1-2. It really is true. God loves the socks off each of us however deep our despair.

God's Time: Psalm 66:19-20. I make time to pray. We can dismiss one of the most treasured gifts that God gives. God stops to listen and to share Himself with us. How precious that is.

God is in the Silence: Psalm 28:1and 6. When I pray yet there is no answer, what do I do? My faith grows as I hold on, when it seems as if God isn't there or isn't really interested in me. God has heard me and validates all I am experiencing. His silence can be affirming.

Grains of Sand: Matthew 6:30-34. The Bible tells us that God knows us intimately, even counting the number of hairs on our head. Often I am keen to tell God what I want Him to do and haven't appreciated that He already knows. God works abundantly and uniquely in each of us, if we will let Him.

Hope: Psalm 61:1-2. When I reach out to God I discover He never fails and is totally trustworthy. If only I were more constant in keeping company with God, especially when the demands of life crowd in.

Hurt: Psalm 103:3. I tend to brood inwardly when emotionally wounded. I may want to justify injury by bitterly rehearsing deeds done to me or words inflicted. God asks me to let it all go to Him and be healed.

I AM: John 11:25-26. A friend figured that he had God in a little box and didn't need Him. One day in his workshop, he literally felt God tapping him on the shoulder and saying, "I AM." All his arguments against belief melted away and he found God waiting for him. God is there in every aspect of our lives.

Janus: Joshua 24:14. Janus was a Roman god of two faces looking in opposite directions, encapsulating for me choices and responses.

Like Grass: John 3:7-8. On the island of Iona, I watched the wind blow through the tall sweep of vegetation, imaging I could also be touched and blown by the Spirit if I am willing.

Mind the Gap: Isaiah 26:8. Waiting is tough particularly when life doesn't change. Yet there is so much that God can teach us and lead us into during such times if we wait on Him.

Openness: Ephesians 3:16-21. Can I trust God and be close to Him? Yes. I am learning to be open to what God wants to do in my life. I am genuinely excited about the 'immeasurably more' God delights to do in us and through us.

Rose: Isaiah 62:3. I watched a beautiful rose gradually flower in the depths of winter. Despite our hardships, it is possible to blossom and beautify the world around us.

Seeing in the Dark: 1 Corinthians 13: 12. Written when the stuff of life threw me into utter chaos. I had no security. There was no way ahead. Your darkness may be that of fear, or guilt or despair. I'm glad that we don't know what lies ahead, but am so grateful that we can find God in it all, in the mess and the muddle, however bleak things are.

Stay Close: Psalm 73:23-24. I am often impatient with a situation and want to run ahead of God, coming up with my schemes and plans. I recognize this is my need to do something, however, I have discovered listening and waiting for God is essential.

Stay with us Lord: Luke 24:29-31. Attending evening prayer in Iona Abbey, I embraced a unique atmosphere of candlelight, ancient stones and music. I felt enveloped in God's presence.

The Cup: Psalm 23:4. Professionally caring for others and walking in shared pain and turmoil, resulted in penning these words. There are a vast range of reactions to devastating illness, such as shock, disbelief, anger (at others), withdrawal or stoicism. God is not remote but there to share the journey with us.

The Gift: Psalm 118:24. Today is the gift we have each been given. How will I live it?

The Lake: Psalm 62:5. This is the first poem which I wrote. I woke early on a holiday and walked to the lakeside to spend time alone with God and allow His creation to speak. This is what He said to me.

The Oyster Pearl: Romans 8:28. A pearl may be formed from grit inside the oyster shell. The oyster no longer is solely for consumption but is prized and sought after for the treasure within. How deeply God can work to lovingly change us on the inside.

The Path: Isaiah 41:10. The Devon coastal path is very undulating. I enjoy the downhill but before long it is all uphill and rather hard work. My life seems uphill; I can feel weary and worn down, but I recognize God is there with me as I dig in deep.

The Peace of God: Isaiah 26:3. Peace may be found in quietness, but how transforming it is to know peace in the storms of life.

The Pebble: Philippians 1:6. A friend picked up a beautiful pebble on the beach as we walked. It had been so worn by many seas that it had become utterly smooth and polished. It was pleasurable to hold, pondering on all that small stone had endured. The greater wonder is that God, through His Spirit, continues to fashion us to His image. He never gives up on us.

The Sea: Psalm 95:3-5. I love watching the waves, the tide turning, indeed the majesty and power of God's creation. I can identify my thoughts and feelings in creation's moods.

Walk Slowly: Psalm 34:18. Loss changes us for ever. There is no time-scale of change, so don't rush, be kind and love yourself in the roller-coaster of emotions. Self-care is not selfish.

Where is my Hope? Jeremiah 29:11. The rainbow of hope was a symbol to inspire during the pandemic. God paints a picture of what hope in Him means.

Will You Hold My Hand? 2 Corinthians 12:9. As my mother lived her final days I was at her bedside, literally holding her hand. The opportunity afforded reflection on the way mum had lived her life and how she had learnt to receive God's grace in and through all her days, even in her final struggles.

Will You Love Me? Psalm 55:22. I was given the diagnosis of cancer just prior to coronavirus lock-down. Isolated and facing an unknown future, I discovered God to be always seeking a relationship, however grim the circumstances that may shrink our capacity to reach out to Him.